Cambridge Young Learners English Tests

Cambridge Movers

Answer Booklet

Examination papers from the

University of Cambridge
Local Examinations Syndicate

CAMBRIDGE
UNIVERSITY PRESS

PUBLISHED BY THE PRESS SYNDICATE OF THE UNIVERSITY OF CAMBRIDGE
The Pitt Building, Trumpington Street, Cambridge CB2 1RP, United Kingdom

CAMBRIDGE UNIVERSITY PRESS
The Edinburgh Building, Cambridge CB2 2RU, United Kingdom
40 West 20th Street, New York, NY 10011-4211, USA
10 Stamford Road, Oakleigh, Melbourne 3166, Australia

Printed in the United Kingdom at the University Press, Cambridge

ISBN 0 521 65903 5 Student's Book
ISBN 0 521 66765 8 Answer Booklet
ISBN 0 521 65900 0 Cassette

Contents

Introduction

The *Cambridge Young Learners English Tests* offer an elementary-level testing system for learners of English between the ages of 7 and 12. The tests include 3 key levels of assessment: *Starters*, *Movers* and *Flyers*. However, this is very general, and there is likely to be considerable variation from country to country.

Test instructions are very simple, and consist of words and structures specified in the syllabus.

Movers is the second level in the series and is designed for children aged between 7 and 11, who have completed about 175 hours of learning.

The complete test lasts about an hour, and has the following components:

	length	number of parts	number of items
Listening	25 minutes	5	25
Reading and Writing	30 minutes	6	40
Speaking	7 minutes	4	–

Candidates need a pen or pencil for the Reading and Writing paper, and coloured pens or pencils for the Listening paper. All answers are written on the question papers.

Listening

In general, the aim is to focus on the 'here and now' and to use language in meaningful contexts. In addition to multiple choice and short answer questions, candidates are asked to use coloured pencils to mark their responses to some tasks. There are 4 parts. Each part begins with a clear example.

Part	skill focus	input	expected response	number of items
1	listening for lexical items and verb phrases	picture and dialogue	match names to a picture by drawing lines	5
2	listening for specified information	gapped text and dialogue	record words or numbers	5
3	listening for lexical items and verb phrases (past tense)	pictures, days of the week and dialogue	match days of the week to pictures by copying the name	5
4	listening for lexical items	picture sets and dialogue	select 1 of 3 pictures by ticking a box	5
5	listening for specified information	picture and dialogue	colour and draw	5

Reading and Writing

Again, the focus is on the 'here and now' and the use of language in meaningful contexts where possible. To complete the test, candidates need a single pen or pencil of any colour. There are 6 parts, each starting with a clear example.

Part	skill focus	input	expected response	number of items
1	understanding definitions	labelled pictures and definitions	matching definitions to a picture by copying a word	6
2	understanding short texts	picture and short texts	write 'yes' or 'no' next to the texts	6
3	identifying appropriate utterances	short dialogues with multiple responses	select best response by writing a letter in a box	6
4	completing a gapped text with 1 word	gapped text with picture cues	write words in gaps	7
5	answering open-ended questions	text, pictures and questions	write 1 – 3 words	10
6	completing a gapped text with 1 word	gapped text and word sets	complete text by selecting the best word and copying	5

Speaking

In the Speaking test, the candidate speaks with 1 examiner for about 7 minutes. The format of the test is explained in advance to the child in their native language, by a teacher or person familiar to them. This person then takes the child into the exam room and introduces them to the examiner.

The mark for the Speaking paper is for interactive listening ability, pronunciation and production of words and phrases.

Part	input	expected response
1	greeting and name check; 2 similar pictures	identify 4 differences between pictures
2	picture sequence	relate the story
3	picture sets	identify the odd one out and give reason
4	open-ended questions	answer questions

Further information

The topics, structures, words and tasks upon which *Cambridge Young Learners English Tests* are based are comprehensively described in the handbook, so teachers or parents can know exactly what to expect. More information about the *Cambridge Young Learners English Tests* can be obtained from the Local Secretary for UCLES examinations in your area, or from:

EFL Division (YLE Subject Officer)
UCLES
1 Hills Road
Cambridge
CB1 2EU
United Kingdom

Telephone: +44 1223 553997
Fax: +44 1223 460278

Test 1 Answers

Listening

Part 1

There should be a line between:
1 Paul and the boy under the tree eating a banana
2 John and the boy giving an apple to the horse
3 Jill and the girl holding a rabbit
4 Sally and the girl chasing the sheep
5 Jane and the girl drawing

Part 2

1 7 Main Street   2 4b   3 hockey   4 comics   5 snake

Part 3

Sunday   Thursday   Tuesday
Saturday   Monday   Wednesday

Part 4

1 ☑ ☐ ☐   2 ☐ ☐ ☑   3 ☐ ☐ ☑
4 ☐ ☑ ☐   5 ☐ ☐ ☑

Part 5

1 The big cupboard: green, the small cupboard: yellow
2 There should be a lamp on the table by the bed
3 The boy standing up: red T-shirt
4 The mat in front of the door: brown
5 There should be a red toy plane between the boys

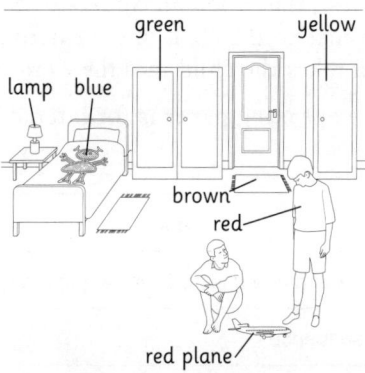

Transcript   *Hello. This is the University of Cambridge Movers Practice Listening Test 1.*

Look at Part 1. Look at the picture.

[pause]

Listen and look. There is one example.

Man: Hello, is Fred at the farm today?
Woman: Yes, I think he's looking at the ducks.
Man: Is he wearing blue trousers?
Woman: Yes, that's Fred.
Man: That's good. He loves ducks.

[pause]

Can you see the line? This is an example. Now you listen and draw lines.

1
Man: Where's Paul?
Woman: He's sitting under the tree with his friend.
Man: There are two boys under the tree. Which one is Paul?
Woman: He's eating a banana.
Man: Oh yes! I can see him now.

[pause]

2
Man: I'm looking for John. Can you see him?
Woman: What's he wearing today?
Man: A green T-shirt, I think.
Woman: Oh yes. He's giving an apple to the horse.

[pause]

3
Man: Look at Jill.
Woman: I can't see her. Where is she?
Man: She's sitting with her friend.
Woman: Has she got a rabbit?
Man: Yes and it's very beautiful.

[pause]

4

Woman: Can you see Sally?
Man: Yes I can. She's running.
Woman: Where? I can't see her.
Man: She's running after that sheep.
Woman: Oh yes, but she can't catch it!

[pause]

5

Woman: Is that Jane sitting on the grass?
Man: With blonde hair?
Woman: What's she doing?
Man: She's trying to draw a picture.
Woman: Oh, she's drawing very carefully.

[pause]

Now listen to Part 1 again.

[The recording is repeated.]

That is the end of Part 1.

Part 2   [pause]

Listen and look. There is one example.

Man: Hello Jill. Can I ask you some questions?
Girl: OK.
Man: What's your family name?
Girl: My family name's Walker.
Man: Jill Walker. Can you spell that?
Girl: W–A–L–K–E–R.
Man: Thank you.

[pause]

Can you see the answer?
Now you listen and write.

1

Man: Where do you live Jill?
Girl: I live at 7 Main Street.
Man: Can you spell that please?
Girl: Yes M–A–I–N.

[pause]

2

Man: Do you like school Jill?
Girl: Yes, I do.
Man: Which class are you in?
Girl: I'm in 4b. I've got a lot of friends in the class.
Man: 4b.

[pause]

3

Man: And what about sports?
Girl: Oh I love swimming, hockey and basketball.
Man: Which is your favourite sport?
Girl: I love hockey best.
Man: Hockey's a good game.

[pause]

4

Man: What do you do at the weekends?
Girl: I have a lot of hobbies. But I like reading best.
Man: Do you like reading books or comics?
Girl: Mmmm... that's difficult. I think comics are my favourite.

[pause]

5

Man: Have you got any pets?
Girl: Yes, I have. I love animals.
Man: What kind of pet have you got?
Girl: I've got a snake. He's very beautiful.
Man: A snake! That's a good pet.

[pause]

Now listen to Part 2 again.

[The recording is repeated.]

That is the end of Part 2.

Part 3   *Look at the pictures. What did Jane do last week?*

[pause]

Listen and look. There is one example.

Boy: Where were you on Thursday Jane?
Girl: I was at my friend's house.
Boy: Did you have tea with her?
Girl: Yes, it was a very good tea. It was her birthday party and she had a beautiful cake.

[pause]

Can you see the word 'Thursday'?
On Thursday Jane went to a birthday party at her friend's house.
Now you listen and write the days.

1

Boy: What did you do on Tuesday?
Girl: I think I was at home on Tuesday.
Boy: Did you watch TV? There was a very good film.
Girl: No, I had to do my homework. I had a lot of homework on Tuesday.
Boy: Did you draw some pictures?
Girl: No, I had to write some sentences in English. It was difficult.

[pause]

2

Boy: What about Saturday? What did you do then?
Girl: I don't know. Oh yes, I watched a soccer game.
Boy: With your friends?
Girl: No, I went to a game with my dad. We watched my brothers play.

Boy: Was it a good game?
Girl: Yes, very good.

[pause]

3

Boy: Did you go to the park on Monday?
Girl: No, I didn't. I had a bad cold.
Boy: What did you do?
Girl: I read my new book. My mum gave it to me for my birthday.
Boy: What's it about?
Girl: A boy and a girl who find a waterfall in a forest.

[pause]

4

Boy: What did you do on Sunday?
Girl: I went to the country.
Boy: With your mum and dad?
Girl: Yes. We had a walk next to a river and we saw a beautiful waterfall.
Boy: Did you swim?
Girl: No, the water was very cold!

[pause]

5

Boy: What about Wednesday?
Girl: Oh yes. I went to the park with my mum and dad.
Boy: Did you play soccer?
Girl: No. Dad and I played a ball game – catch and throw.
Boy: What about your mum?
Girl: She doesn't like ball games. She read a book.

[pause]

Now listen to Part 3 again.

[The recording is repeated.]

That is the end of Part 3.

Part 4 *Look at the pictures.*

[pause]

Listen and look. There is one example. What is Jill wearing?

[pause]

Girl: Look mum, can you see my friend Jill?
Woman: No, I can't. What's she wearing? Red trousers?
Girl: No. She's got a new dress.
Woman: Is it blue?
Girl: No, it's yellow.

[pause]

Can you see the tick?
Now you listen and tick the box.

1 What does Daisy want for supper?

[pause]

Girl: I'm hungry Mum.
Woman: What would you like for supper Daisy, a burger?
Girl: No, I had a burger at school today. Can I have some pasta?
Woman: Yes, with some juice and bread?
Girl: I'm thirsty but I don't want any bread.

[pause]

2 What did Sally get for her birthday?

[pause]

Girl: It was Sally's birthday last week.
Woman: Oh, what did her parents give her?
Girl: I don't know.
Woman: She wanted a guitar or a computer.
Girl: Well they didn't give her those. Oh yes, I know. They gave her a new camera.
Woman: She'll like that. She loves taking photos.

[pause]

3 Where did Peter go at the weekend?

[pause]

Woman: Where did your friend Peter go at the weekend?
Girl: Well, he wanted to go and watch a basketball game.
Woman: So did he go?
Girl: No, he couldn't. His mum wanted to go to the mountains for the weekend and his dad wanted to go to the sea.
Woman: Did he go to the sea then?
Girl: No, his dad had to work but he went with his mum to the mountains.

[pause]

4 What was the matter with Mary?

[pause]

Girl: Mary couldn't come to school today.
Woman: What was the matter with her? Did she have a stomach ache?
Girl: No, she had a temperature.
Woman: Was she in bed?
Girl: No, she sat on the sofa in the living room.

[pause]

5 What fruit has Fred got in his garden?

[pause]

Girl: Mum, Fred's parents have got a new house in the country. It's very big.
Woman: That's good. Has it got a garden?
Girl: Yes, it has, and there's a lot of fruit.
Woman: Oh. Does it have coconuts or bananas?
Girl: No, but it's got a lot of pineapples.

[pause]

Now listen to Part 4 again.

[The recording is repeated.]

That is the end of Part 4.

Part 5   *Look at the picture.*

[pause]

Listen and look. There is one example.

Woman: Can you see the monster on the bed?
Boy: Yes I can.
Woman: Well, colour the monster blue.

[pause]

Can you see the blue monster?
Now you listen and colour and draw.

1

Woman: There are two cupboards in the room. Can you see them?
Boy: Yes, a big one and a smaller one.
Woman: I want you to colour them.
Boy: What colour?
Woman: Colour the big cupboard green and the smaller one yellow.
Boy: OK.

[pause]

2

Woman: Now I want you to draw something.
Boy: Good. What shall I draw?
Woman: Draw a lamp.
Boy: Where?
Woman: On the small table next to the bed.
Boy: OK.

[pause]

3

Woman: Now you can colour again.
Boy: Good.
Woman: Can you see the two boys?
Boy: Yes, I can see them.
Woman: Colour the boy who's standing.
Boy: Shall I colour his trousers?
Woman: No, colour his T-shirt red.
Boy: OK, his T-shirt.

[pause]

4

Woman: Do you want to colour again?
Boy: Yes please.
Woman: OK. You can colour the mat on the floor.
Boy: Which one? There are two.
Woman: Colour the one in front of the door.
Boy: What colour?
Woman: Brown.
Boy: OK.

[pause]

5

Woman: And now you can draw again.
Boy: Good. What shall I draw?
Woman: The boys need something to play with.
Boy: Shall I draw a car or a plane?
Woman: A plane, that's good.
Boy: Where?
Woman: Draw a plane between the boys and then colour it red.

[pause]

Now listen to Part 5 again.

[The recording is repeated.]

That is the end of the Movers Practice Listening Test 1.

Reading and Writing

Part 1

1 (a) map   2 (a) playground   3 (a) library
4 blankets   5 towels   6 homework

Part 2

1 yes   2 yes   3 no   4 yes   5 no   6 no

Part 3

1 A   2 C   3 B   4 A   5 B   6 B

Part 4

1 pirate   2 sailed   3 island   4 box
5 treasure   6 Look   7 An afternoon with Dad

Part 5

1 a bag   2 the supermarket   3 fruit and bread
4 below the pasta   5 she isn't tall
6 she jumped (down)   7 her leg   8 an ice cream
9 her dad   10 in his car/in the car/by car/in Dad's car

Part 6

1 and   2 than   3 sometimes
4 with   5 in   6 are

Speaking

Part	Usher/Examiner does this:	Examiner says this:	Response expected from child:	Back-up questions:
	usher brings candidate in. Usher settles candidate in, using L1, then says to Examiner, **Hello, this is Daniel**.	Hello, *Daniel*, my name's *Jane*. How old are you?	Hello. *8*.	Are you 8? 9?
1	points to Find the Difference card.	**Look at these pictures. They look the same but some things are different. There is a pirate on this island, but there is a monster on this island. What other different things can you see?**	describes four other differences: – red boat/blue boat – 1 tree/2 trees – monkey under/in tree – it's raining/a sunny day	point to other differences the candidate does not mention. Give one half of a suitable response e.g. **This boat is red but …**
2	points to Story card. points at the other pictures.	**Now look at these pictures. They show a story. Look at the first one.** "A cat and an old woman are sleeping in the garden." **Now you tell the story.**	(many variations possible) **The cat's afraid. It's climbing the tree. Now the cat can't climb down. The old woman can't help it. She's phoning. The man in the helicopter is helping the cat. The old woman is very happy.**	questions to prompt other parts of the story: **What is the cat doing? Why? What can't the cat do now? What is the old woman doing? What is the man in the helicopter doing? Is the old woman happy?**
3	points to Find the Different Ones card. Points to Sets 1, 2 and 3 in turn.	**Now look at these pictures. This one is different. A banana, an orange and a pineapple are all fruit. This isn't a fruit. It's a cake. Now you tell me. Which one is different? (Why?)**	student suggests a difference – it does not, of course, matter if their difference is not the most predictable one.	Set 1 (pointing at steak burger and chicken) **Are these meat? And** (pointing at ice cream) **what about this?** Set 2 **What do you do with these? And this?** Set 3 **Where do these animals live? And this?**
4	puts away all pictures.	**Now let's talk about your hobbies. What sports do you like? When do you play football? What do you like doing at home? Tell me about the weekends.**	*football* *Saturday* *watching TV* *I play with my friends and go to the cinema.*	Do you like football? Do you play on Saturday? Do you like watching TV? Do you play with your friends?
		OK, thank you, *Daniel*. Good-bye.	**Good-bye.**	

Test 2 Answers

Listening

Part 1

There should be a line between:

1 Tom and the boy drawing a car on the board
2 Jane and the girl playing with a toy bus
3 Paul and the boy drawing a house on the board
4 Anna and the girl holding a toy plane
5 Pat and the girl sitting in front of the computer

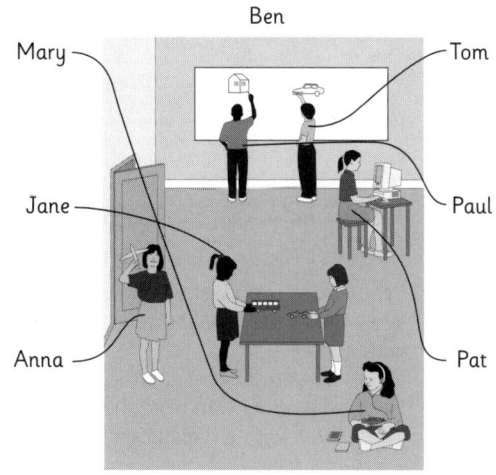

Part 2

1 9   2 blonde   3 blue   4 3   5 4

Part 3

Tuesday   Friday   Wednesday
Sunday   Saturday   Thursday

Part 4

1 ☐ ☐ ✓   2 ☐ ☐ ✓   3 ✓ ☐ ☐
4 ☐ ☐ ✓   5 ☐ ✓ ☐

Part 5

1 The fat man's T-shirt: red and the thin man's
  T-shirt: yellow
2 There should be a duck swimming in the pond.
3 smaller car: green
4 There should be a big black cloud above the
  two men.
5 biggest dog: brown

*Part 5
(cont.)*

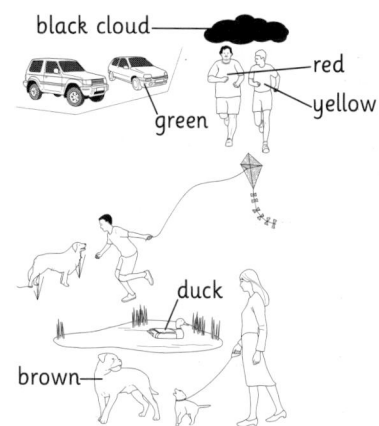

TRANSCRIPT   *Hello. This is the University of
Cambridge Movers Practice Listening
Test 2.*

Look at Part 1. Look at the picture.

[pause]

Listen and look. There is one example.

Man: Hello, is Mary here?
Woman: Yes, she's listening to a CD.
Man: Is she wearing a red skirt?
Woman: Yes, that's Mary. She loves music.

[pause]

*Can you see the line? This is an
example. Now you listen and
draw lines.*

1

Man: Where's Tom?
Woman: He's drawing a picture on the board.
Man: There are two boys drawing. Which
          one is Tom?
Woman: He's drawing a car.
Man: Oh yes! I can see him now.

[pause]

2

Man: Where's Jane?
Woman: She's playing with a toy.
Man: Is she playing with a toy plane?
Woman: No, she's playing with a bus.
Man: Oh yes, I can see her.

[pause]

3

Man: I'm looking for Paul. Can you see him?
Woman: What's he wearing today?
Man: Black trousers, I think.
Woman: Oh yes, he's standing at the board.
Man: I see. He's drawing a house.

[pause]

4

Woman:	Look at Anna.
Man:	Where is she?
Woman:	She's standing by the door.
Man:	Is she wearing a red T-shirt?
Woman:	Yes, she is and she's got a toy plane.

[pause]

5

Woman:	Can you see Pat?
Man:	Yes, I can. She's working.
Woman:	What's she doing?
Man:	She's working at the computer.
Woman:	Oh yes, she likes that.

[pause]

Now listen to Part 1 again.

[The recording is repeated.]

That is the end of Part 1.

Part 2 [pause]

Listen and look. There is one example.

Man:	Hello Mary. Can I ask you some questions?
Girl:	All right.
Man:	What's your family name?
Girl:	Do you mean Mary?
Man:	No, your second name?
Girl:	Oh that's Smith.
Man:	Is that S–M–I–T–H?
Girl:	Yes.

[pause]

Can you see the answer?
Now you listen and write.

1

Man:	And how old are you Mary?
Girl:	I'm 9. It was my birthday last week.
Man:	Did you have a party?
Girl:	Yes, it was good.

[pause]

2

Man:	Now what about your hair?
Girl:	My hair?
Man:	Yes, what colour is it?
Girl:	It's blonde.

[pause]

3

Man:	And what about your eyes?
Girl:	Do you need to know the colour of my eyes?
Man:	Yes please.
Girl:	They're blue.
Man:	You've got very beautiful eyes, Mary!
Girl:	Thank you!

[pause]

4

Man:	Now some questions about your family. Is that OK?
Girl:	Yes, it's OK.
Man:	Have you got any brothers?
Girl:	Yes, I've got three brothers. Two are older than me and one is younger.
Man:	That's a big family.
Girl:	I like big families.

[pause]

5

Man:	What about sisters? How many sisters have you got?
Girl:	Four. There are a lot of people in our house!

[pause]

Now listen to Part 2 again.

[The recording is repeated.]

That is the end of Part 2.

Part 3 *Look at the pictures. What did Paul do last week?*

[pause]

Listen and look. There is one example.

Girl:	What did you do last week Paul?
Boy:	Well, last week I played a lot of sport. It was good.
Girl:	What did you do on Tuesday?
Boy:	I played hockey with my school on Tuesday. It was a difficult game.

[pause]

Can you see the word 'Tuesday'?
On Tuesday Paul played hockey with his school.
Now you listen and write the days.

1

Girl:	What did you do on Thursday?
Boy:	I watched basketball.
Girl:	At school?
Boy:	No, I watched it on TV. It was very good.

[pause]

2

Girl:	What about Friday? What did you do on Friday?
Boy:	Oh, on Friday I usually go swimming, but last Friday it was a friend's birthday party.
Girl:	Did you go to his house?
Boy:	No, we went skating with his Dad.
Girl:	Did you like it?
Boy:	Yes, very much.

[pause]

3

Girl: What did you do on Wednesday?
Boy: I went swimming with Dad, I think.
Girl: Can you swim well?
Boy: Yes, but Dad swims faster than me.

[pause]

4

Girl: What did you do on Saturday?
Boy: Oh it was basketball again.
Girl: Another game on TV?
Boy: No I played at my school on Saturday. Basketball's my favourite sport.

[pause]

5

Girl: So what sport did you play on Sunday?
Boy: Nothing.
Girl: Why not?
Boy: I was tired. I slept all day.

[pause]

Now listen to Part 3 again.

[The recording is repeated.]

That is the end of Part 3.

Part 4   *Look at the pictures.*

[pause]

Listen and look. There is one example. Where is Pat's dad going?

Boy: Is that your father walking to the bus stop Pat?
Girl: Yes, it is Sam.
Boy: Where's he going?
Girl: He's going to town for Mum.
Boy: Is he going to the supermarket?
Girl: No, I went there yesterday and Mum's going to the library this afternoon. Oh, I know, he's going to the bank.

[pause]

Can you see the tick?
Now you listen and tick the box.

1 Which one is Pat's mother?

[pause]

Boy: Is your mother here Pat?
Girl: Yes, she's in the garden with my aunts.
Boy: Has your mother got straight hair?
Girl: No, her hair is curly.
Boy: Oh, is she the one in the red dress?
Girl: No, she's wearing trousers today.

[pause]

2 What does Pat want to buy?

[pause]

Boy: Where are you going to go now Pat?
Girl: I'm going shopping.
Boy: What do you want to buy?
Girl: It's my birthday on Sunday and I want something new to wear at my party.
Boy: Do you want some new trousers?
Girl: No, I'd like a skirt because Mum gave me a beautiful blue sweater.

[pause]

3 What was the weather like here yesterday?

[pause]

Boy: We went to the mountains yesterday and it rained. What was the weather like here Pat?
Girl: It was a beautiful day.
Boy: Was it sunny?
Girl: It was sunny. It wasn't cloudy at all.

[pause]

4 Where's Peter?

[pause]

Boy: Where's your brother Pat?
Girl: Peter? I think he's playing outside.
Boy: Is he in the garden?
Girl: No, he isn't.
Boy: He isn't on the balcony.
Girl: I know. He went to the playground with his friends.

[pause]

5 What will they take on the picnic?

[pause]

Boy: What do you want to eat on our picnic tomorrow Pat?
Girl: Something we can eat with our hands.
Boy: What about sandwiches?
Girl: No, we always take sandwiches. Can we take burgers?
Boy: I don't like cold burgers. Shall we take sausages?
Girl: OK.

[pause]

Now listen to Part 4 again.

[The recording is repeated.]

That is the end of Part 4.

Part 5 Look at the picture.

[pause]

Listen and look. There is one example.

Woman: Can you see the boy with the kite?
Boy: Yes I can see him.
Woman: Well, colour the kite blue.
Boy: The kite?
Woman: That's right.

[pause]

Can you see the blue kite?
Now you listen and colour and draw.

1

Woman: There are two men running in the park. Can you see them?
Boy: Yes, a thin man and a fat man.
Woman: I want you to colour their T-shirts.
Boy: What colour?
Woman: Colour the fat man's T-shirt red and the thin man's yellow.
Boy: OK.

[pause]

2

Woman: Now I want you to draw something.
Boy: Good. What shall I draw?
Woman: Can you draw a duck?
Boy: Yes, I can!
Woman: Good. Well, draw a duck swimming in the water.
Boy: OK.

[pause]

3

Woman: Now you can colour again.
Boy: Good.
Woman: Can you see the two cars?
Boy: Yes, shall I colour the small car or the big car?
Woman: Colour the smaller one green.
Boy: OK. I like that colour.

[pause]

4

Woman: Now you can draw something again.
Boy: Good.
Woman: What about the weather?
Boy: It's a cold day so shall I draw a big cloud?
Woman: Yes, draw a big cloud above the two men, and colour it black.

[pause]

5

Woman: Now I want you to colour one more thing.
Boy: Good. What shall I colour?
Woman: The dog please.
Boy: Which one?
Woman: Colour the biggest dog brown.
Boy: There you are.
Woman: That's very good.

[pause]

Now listen to Part 5 again.

[The recording is repeated.]

That is the end of the Movers Practice Listening Test 2.

Reading and Writing

Part 1

1 CDs   2 videos   3 soup   4 (a) shark   5 coffee
6 (a) sandwich

Part 2

1 yes   2 yes   3 no   4 no   5 no   6 yes

Part 3

1 B   2 C   3 A   4 C   5 B   6 A

Part 4

1 flowers   2 sheep   3 saw   4 swam
5 wet/afraid   6 apple   7 A new friend

Part 5

1 by the sea   2 (swim and) play
3 her mother   4 (number) 20
5 (some) lemonade   6 an old woman
7 it was hot   8 she was afraid
9 Daisy's grandmother   10 some cake

Part 6

1 are   2 they   3 live   4 quickly
5 in   6 them

Speaking

Part	Usher/Examiner does this:	Examiner says this:	Response expected from child:	Back-up questions:
	usher brings candidate in. usher settles candidate in, using L1, then says to Examiner, **Hello, this is Andrea**.	Hello, *Andrea*, my name's *Peter*. How old are you?	Hello. *8*.	Are you 8? 9?
1	points to Find the Difference card.	**Look at these pictures. They look the same but some things are different. This man has a green shirt, but this man has a yellow shirt. What other different things can you see?**	describes four other differences: – 2 pandas/2 kangaroos – 3 children/2 children – tall/short trees – woman wearing/not wearing a hat	point to other differences the candidate does not mention. give one half of a suitable response e.g. **In this picture there are 2 pandas but …**
2	points to Story card.

points at the other pictures. | **Now look at these pictures. They show a story. Look at the first one.**

"The family are on the beach. The children are playing. Their mother is reading." **Now you tell the story.** | (many variations possible)

The father's going into the sea. The mother and the girl are watching him. The father's swimming. He sees a shark. He's afraid. He shouts "Help!" But it isn't a shark. It's the boy. He's laughing, but his father isn't happy. | questions to prompt other parts of the story: **Where is the father going?**

What can he see? Is he afraid? Is there a shark in the sea? Is the father happy? |
| 3 | points to Find the Different Ones card, points to 1, 2 and 3 in turn. | **Now look at these pictures. This one is different. A banana, an orange and a pineapple are all fruit. This isn't a fruit. It's a cake. Now you tell me. Which one is different? Why?** | student suggests a difference – it does not, of course, matter if their difference is not the most predictable one. | Set 1 (pointing at sheep, horse, cow). **How many legs have these got? And** (pointing at the fish) **what about this?** Set 2 **Have these men got hair on their faces? And this one?** Set 3 **Is there water here? And here?** |
| 4 | puts away all pictures. | **Now let's talk about your home. Where do you live? How many rooms are there in your house? Which room do you play in?**

Tell me about your *bedroom*. | *Centro* *5*

bedroom

It's small. It has 2 beds. | **Do you live in** *Centro*? **Have you got 5 rooms in your house? 6? Do you play in your bedroom?**

Is your bedroom big? Small? |
| | | **OK, thank you, *Andrea*, good-bye.** | Good-bye. | |

Test 3 Answers

Listening

Part 1

There should be a line between:

1 Mrs Green and the lady in front of the supermarket wearing a red skirt and a red hat
2 Paul and the boy looking in the toy shop window carrying a school bag
3 Mr Farmer and the man driving the small blue car
4 Tom and the boy sitting on the bench outside the bank
5 Sue and the girl with the two children

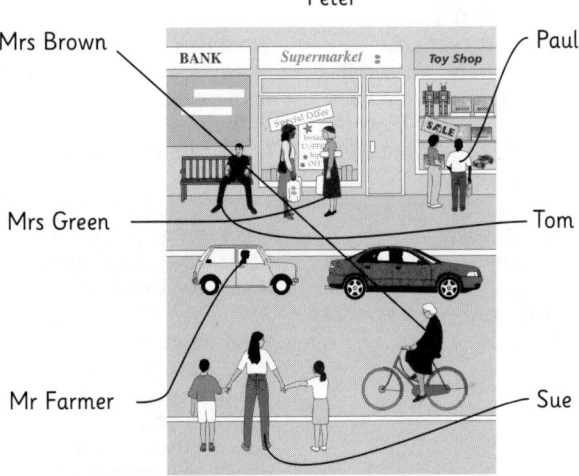

Part 2

1 15 High Street 2 10 3 John 4 Clare
5 neck

Part 3

Friday   Saturday   Wednesday
Sunday   Monday   Tuesday

Part 4

1 ✓ ☐ ☐   2 ☐ ☐ ✓   3 ☐ ✓ ☐
4 ☐ ☐ ✓   5 ✓ ☐ ☐

Part 5

1 the chair in the bathroom: yellow
2 There should be a table in the bedroom between the bed and the cupboard.
3 the cupboards in the kitchen: brown
4 There should be a black cat sleeping on the bed in the bedroom.
5 the mat in the living room: red

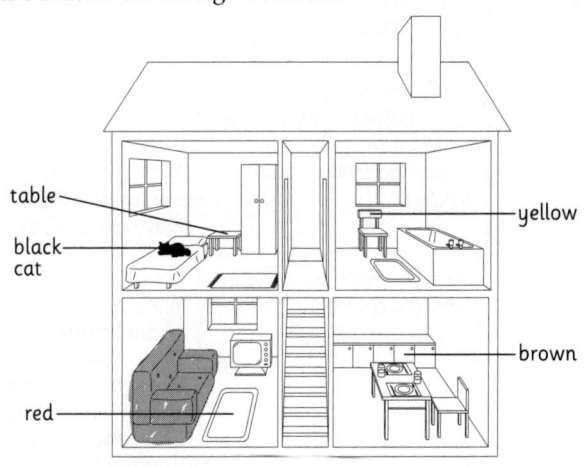

3

Man:	I need to find Mr Farmer. Can you see him?
Woman:	Yes, I can.
Man:	Where is he?
Woman:	He's there in his car.
Man:	Which car?
Woman:	The small blue one.

[pause]

4

Woman:	Look at Tom. He's very tired today.
Man:	Where is he?
Woman:	He's sitting outside the bank.
Man:	Well, he played a lot of tennis yesterday.
Woman:	Yes, that's why he's sitting down now.

[pause]

5

Woman:	Is that Sue?
Man:	Where?
Woman:	Walking with the two children.
Man:	Oh yes, that's Sue, but who are the children?
Woman:	I think they're her cousins.

[pause]

Now listen to Part 1 again.

[The recording is repeated.]

That is the end of Part 1.

Part 2 [pause]

Listen and look. There is one example.

Woman:	Hello Tom. Can I ask you some questions?
Boy:	All right.
Woman:	What's your family name?
Boy:	Hill.
Woman:	Can you spell that?
Boy:	H–I–L–L.
Woman:	Thank you.

[pause]

Can you see the answer?
Now you listen and write.

1

Woman:	And where do you live Tom?
Boy:	15 High Street.
Woman:	Can you spell 'High' please?
Boy:	H–I–G–H.

[pause]

2

Woman:	Now, how old are you Tom?
Boy:	Ten. It was my birthday last week.
Woman:	You're very tall.
Boy:	Yes, all my family are tall.

[pause]

3

Woman:	Now what's your father's name?
Boy:	John, like my older brother.
Woman:	So there are two Johns in the family.
Boy:	Yes.

[pause]

4

Woman:	And your mother's name?
Boy:	It's Clare.
Woman:	Is that C–L–A–R–E?
Boy:	That's right.

[pause]

5

Woman:	Now what's the matter?
Boy:	My neck hurts.
Woman:	Is it very bad?
Boy:	Yes, it hurts a lot.

[pause]

Now listen to Part 2 again.

[The recording is repeated.]

That is the end of Part 2.

Part 3 *Look at the pictures. What did Jim do last week?*

[pause]

Listen and look. There is one example.

Girl:	What did you do last weekend Jim?
Boy:	On Saturday or Sunday?
Girl:	Saturday.
Boy:	I helped my mother. We painted my bedroom.
Girl:	What colour did you paint it?
Boy:	Blue. It's good now.

Can you see the word 'Saturday'?
On Saturday Jim painted his bedroom.
Now you listen and write the days.

1

Girl:	What did you do on Sunday?
Boy:	I went to the country with my dad.
Girl:	Oh, did you have a picnic?
Boy:	No, we sailed a boat on a lake. It was difficult.

[pause]

2

Girl:	What about Monday? What did you do on Monday?
Boy:	Oh, I watched a film at a friend's house.
Girl:	What was the film about?
Boy:	Some people who sailed over the sea.
Girl:	Did you like it?
Boy:	Yes, it was very good.

[pause]

3

Girl: What did you do on Tuesday?
Boy: I went shopping with Mum.
Girl: To the supermarket?
Boy: No we went to the bookshop. We bought a book for Dad's birthday.

[pause]

4

Girl: What did you do on Wednesday?
Boy: I went to the country.
Girl: Did you go sailing again?
Boy: No I had a picnic with a friend and his family and we swam in a river.

[pause]

5

Girl: So what did you do on Friday?
Boy: Shopping.
Girl: Where did you go?
Boy: I went to the supermarket with Mum. That's all.

[pause]

Now listen to Part 3 again.

[pause]

That is the end of Part 3.

Part 4   *Look at the pictures.*

[pause]

Listen and look. There is one example. Which is Ben's brother's car?

Boy: My brother's got a new car.
Girl: Oh which one is it Ben, that small one?
Boy: No, it's a beautiful, big one.
Girl: Is it blue?
Boy: No, his last car was blue. This one's red.

[pause]

Can you see the tick?
Now you listen and tick the box.

1 What sport does Ben's brother do?

[pause]

Girl: What sport does your brother do Ben?
Boy: He plays basketball every weekend.
Girl: Does he like swimming or tennis?
Boy: No, he doesn't.

[pause]

2 Where does Ben's brother work?

[pause]

Girl: Where does your brother work Ben?
Boy: Here in the town.
Girl: Yes, but where? In a school?

Boy: No, he works in the zoo.
Girl: Where's that?
Boy: It's near the library.
Girl: Oh, yes.

[pause]

3 How did Ben go to his grandparents' house?

[pause]

Girl: Did you see your grandparents at the weekend Ben?
Boy: Yes we did. I was very happy.
Girl: Did you go by bus?
Boy: No, the bus is very slow. We flew there.
Girl: Oh, did you?
Boy: Yes, it's quicker than the train.

[pause]

4 What can Ben give his sister for her birthday?

[pause]

Boy: It's my sister's birthday on Saturday. What can I give her Daisy?
Girl: Does she like dolls?
Boy: No, she doesn't.
Girl: What about a dress?
Boy: She never wears dresses. She likes playing football with me.
Girl: You can give her a ball then.
Boy: Oh yes!

[pause]

5 What's Ben's sister's favourite food?

[pause]

Boy: Do you want to come to my sister's birthday party Daisy?
Girl: Thanks. Have you got a birthday cake?
Boy: Yes, but my sister doesn't like cake.
Girl: What's her favourite food, burgers?
Boy: She likes bananas best. She sometimes eats ten every day!

[pause]

Now listen to Part 4 again.

[The recording is repeated.]

That is the end of Part 4.

Part 5   *Look at the picture.*

[pause]

Listen and look. There is one example.

Woman: Can you see the sofa in the living room?
Boy: Yes I can see it.
Woman: Well, colour it green.
Boy: OK.

[pause]

Can you see the green sofa?

Now you listen and colour and draw.

1

Woman: There's a chair in the bathroom. Can you see it?
Boy: Yes, I can.
Woman: I want you to colour it.
Boy: What colour?
Woman: Yellow.
Boy: OK. A yellow chair.

[pause]

2

Woman: Now I want you to draw something.
Boy: Good. What shall I draw?
Woman: Can you draw a table?
Boy: Where?
Woman: In the bedroom. Draw a small table between the bed and the cupboard.
Boy: Shall I draw it now?
Woman: Yes please. That's right. Between the bed and the cupboard.

[pause]

3

Woman: Now you can colour again.
Boy: Good.
Woman: Can you see the cupboards in the kitchen?
Boy: Yes, what colour shall I do?
Woman: Colour them brown please.
Boy: Right.

[pause]

4

Woman: Now you can draw something again.
Boy: Good.
Woman: Can you draw a cat?
Boy: Yes, where?
Woman: In the bedroom. Draw a big, black cat sleeping on the bed.
Boy: Like my cat?
Woman: Yes. That's a beautiful cat!

[pause]

5

Woman: Now I want you to colour one more thing.
Boy: Good. What shall I colour?
Woman: The mat, please.
Boy: Which one?
Woman: In the living room.
Boy: Can I colour it red?
Woman: Yes, that's a good colour for a mat.

[pause]

Now listen to Part 5 again.

[The recording is repeated.]

That is the end of the Movers Practice Listening Test 3.

Reading and Writing

Part 1

1 (a) town   2 mountains   3 (a) bottle
4 (a) farm   5 stairs   6 (the) world

Part 2

1 yes   2 no   3 yes   4 no   5 no   6 yes

Part 3

1 B   2 A   3 B   4 A   5 B   6 C

Part 4

1 downstairs   2 bread   3 bicycle   4 street/town
5 open   6 laughed   7 Jim makes a mistake

Part 5

1 blue and yellow   2 Pasta
3 some words   4 five/5
5 in the living room   6 Mary's brother (Fred)
7 outside   8 Mary and Fred
9 in the kitchen   10 some fruit

Part 6

1 another   2 have   3 There   4 going   5 to

Speaking

Part	Usher/Examiner does this:	Examiner says this:	Response expected from child:	Back-up questions:
	usher brings candidate in, usher settles candidate in, using L1, then says to Examiner, **Hello, this is Anna**.	**Hello, *Anna*, my name's *Mary*. How old are you?**	Hello. *8*	Are you 8? 9?
1	points to Find the Difference card.	**Look at these pictures. They look the same but some things are different. This blanket is yellow, but this blanket is blue. What other different things can you see?**	describes four other differences: – 2/1 chair(s) – car on/under bed – mother/father – drinking/not drinking	point to other differences the candidate does not mention. give one half of a suitable response e.g. **In this picture there are 2 chairs, but …**
2	points to Story card. points at the other pictures.	**Now look at these pictures. They show a story. Look at the first one. "A family is by the river. Mother and father are cooking and the children are fishing. They want a fish for lunch." Now you tell the story.**	(many variations possible) **The girl's saying "Look! He's got a fish!" But the boy hasn't got a fish. He's got an old shoe! He's very sad. But there are 2 small fish inside the shoe. Now the children are very happy.**	questions to prompt other parts of the story: **What's the girl saying?** **Has the boy got a fish?** **What's inside the shoe?** **Are the children happy now?**
3	points to Find the Different Ones card. Points to Sets 1, 2 and 3 in turn.	**Now look at these four pictures. This one is different. A banana, an orange and a pineapple are all fruit. This isn't a fruit. It's a cake. Now you tell me. Which one is different? (Why?)**	student suggests a difference – it does not, of course, matter if their difference is not the most predictable one.	Set 1: (pointing at bird, helicopter, plane) **Do these fly? And** (pointing at monkey) **What about this?** Set 2: **Can you sit on these? And this?** Set 3: **Are these children playing? And these?**
4	puts away all pictures.	**Now let's talk about food. What's your favourite food? What do you eat for breakfast? Where do you have lunch?** **Tell me about your favourite drinks.**	*burgers* *bread* *(at) school* *I like milk in the morning and juice at lunch.*	Do you like burgers? Do you have bread for breakfast? Do you have lunch at school? Do you like milk in the morning?
		OK, thank you, *Anna*. Good-bye.	Good-bye.	

COMBINED STARTERS AND MOVERS THEMATIC VOCABULARY LIST

For ease of reference vocabulary is arranged in semantic groups or themes.

In addition to the topics, notions and concepts listed for the syllabus, the following categories appear:

- miscellaneous objects/nouns
- adjectives
- determiners
- adverbs
- prepositions
- pronouns
- conjunctions
- verbs

s – first appears at Starters

m – first appears at Movers

ANIMALS

s animal
m bat
m bear
s bird
s cat
s chicken
s cow
s crocodile
s dog
m dolphin
s duck
s elephant
s fish (s + pl)
m fly
s frog
s giraffe
s goat
s hippo
s horse
m kangaroo
m lion
s lizard
s monkey
s mouse/mice
m panda
m parrot
m pet
m rabbit
m shark
s sheep (s + pl)
s snake
s spider
s tiger
m whale

THE BODY AND THE FACE

s arm
m back
m beard
m blonde
s body
m curly
s ear
s eye
s face
m fair
s foot/feet
s hair
s hand
s head
s leg
m moustache
s mouth
m neck
s nose
m shoulder
m stomach
m straight
m tooth/teeth

CLOTHES

s clothes
m coat
s dress
s glasses
s handbag
s hat
s jacket
s jeans
m scarf
s shirt
s shoe
s skirt
s sock
m sweater
s T-shirt
s trousers
s wear

FAMILY, FRIENDS AND OURSELVES

s Ann
m Anna
m aunt
s baby
s Ben
s picture
s play (with)
s radio
s read

s run
s sing
s soccer
s song
s story
s swim
s table tennis
s television/TV
s tennis
s toy
m video
s watch

LOCAL PLACES

m bank
m bus station
m cinema
m farm
m hospital
m library
m market
m park
m playground
m shop
m supermarket
m zoo

WORK

m clown
m pirate
m work

SCHOOL AND THE CLASSROOM, AND LANGUAGE AND TESTS

s alphabet
s answer
s ask
s board
s book
s bookcase
s class
s classroom
s close
s colour
s colour (in)
s correct
s cross
s desk
s draw
s English
s eraser
s example

s find
s floor
m homework
s know (don't know)
s learn
s lesson
s letter
s line
s listen (to)
s look
m mistake
s no
s number
s open
s page
s part
s pen
s pencil
s picture
m playground
s question
s read
s right
s ruler
s school
s sentence
s teacher
s tell
s test
m text
s tick
s understand
s wall
s word
s write
s yes

TRANSPORT

s bike
s boat
s bus
s car
s fly
s go
s helicopter
s motorbike
s plane
s ride
s run
s swim
s train
s walk

COLOURS

s black
s blue
s brown
s green
s grey (or gray)
s pink
s purple
s red
s white
s yellow

LOCATION AND POSITION

s at
s behind
s between
s here
s in
s in front of
s next to
s on
s there
s under

WEATHER

m cloud(y)
m rain
m rainbow
m snow
m sunny
m weather
m windy

THE WORLD AROUND US

m city
m country(side)
m field
m forest
m grass
m island
m jungle
m lake
m leaf/leaves
m moon
m mountain
m plant
m river
m road
m rock
m star
m town
m village

m waterfall
m world

MISCELLANEOUS OBJECTS/NOUNS

s bag
m blanket
m bottom
s box
s computer
s day
m difference
m fan
m kind (=type)
m map
s monster
s night
m place
s robot
s sea
s sun
m thing
m toothbrush
m top
m towel
m treasure
m wash

NUMBERS

m Ordinals: 1–20
m Cardinals: 1st–10th

CONTAINERS

m bottle (of)
m bowl (of)
m cup (of)
m glass (of)

TIME EXPRESSIONS

m after
m afternoon
m always
m before
m evening
m every
m never
m sometimes
m week
m weekend
m yesterday
The days of the week:
m Monday
m Tuesday
m Wednesday
m Thursday
m Friday
m Saturday
m Sunday

GREETINGS AND OTHER FORMULAIC EXPRESSIONS

s bye (-bye)
m excuse me!
m good morning/afternoon/evening/night
s good-bye
m Great!
s hello
m I didn't understand/hear you
s I don't know
s no
s oh
s OK
s pardon
s please
s right
s so
s sorry
s thank you
s then
s well
m What did you say?
m What's the matter?
s yes

ADJECTIVES

m afraid
m bad
s beautiful
m best
m better
s big
m careful
s clean
m cold
m different
m difficult
s dirty
m easy
m famous
m fat
s favourite
s good
s happy
m hot
m hungry
m loud
s new
s old
m quick
m quiet
s right
m round
s sad
m slow
s small
m square
m strong
m tall
m thin
m thirsty
m tired
s ugly
m weak
m well
m wet
m worse
m worst
m wrong
s young

DETERMINERS

s a/an
m all
m another
m any
m every
s no
s that
s the
s these
s this
s those

ADVERBS

m a little
m well
m upstairs
m up
m then
m sometimes
m slowly
m quietly
m quickly
m outside
m out
m often
m off
m loudly
m inside
m downstairs

m down
m carefully
m badly
m always
m a lot
s again
s here
s now
s there
s today
s very

PREPOSITIONS

m about
m above
m after
s at
m before
s behind
m below
s between
s in
s in front of
m inside
s like
s next to
s of
s on
m on (time)
m opposite
m outside
s to
s under

PRONOUNS

m all
m mine
m nothing
m ours
m something
m theirs

CONJUNCTIONS

m because
m but
m than

VERBS

Irregular:
s be
m buy
s can/cannot/can't
s catch
m choose
m come
s do/don't
s draw
s drink
s eat
s find
s fly
m get (un)dressed
m get up
s give
s go
s have (got)
m have (got) to
m hurt
s know
s learn
s put
m mean
m must
m put on
s read
s ride
s run
s say
s sing
s sit (down)
s sleep
s spell
s stand (up)
s swim
m take
m take off
m take pictures
s throw
s understand
m wake up
s wear
s write

Regular:
s answer

s ask
m carry
s close
m clean
m climb
s colour
m cook
s cross
m cry
m dance
s enjoy
m fish
m help
m hop
s jump
s kick
m laugh
s learn
s like
s listen (to)
s live
s look
s love
s open
s paint
s phone
s pick up
s play (with)
s point
m need
m sail
m shop
m shout
s show
m shower
m skate
s start
s stop
s talk
s tick
s try
s walk
m wait
s want
s watch
m wash
m work